Page 1: Title Page
Logan's life story
By Logan Keener
Page 2: Copyright Page
Copyright © Logan Keener 2024 - Introduction

Table of contents - Introduction
- Chapter 1: The Beginning
- Chapter 2: Navigating Mental Health - Chapter 3: Kaiser Bear Keener: My Emotional Support
- Chapter 4: Therapy and Support
- Chapter 5: School Experiences
Beginning Early experiences with autism, family dynamics, and the journey towards diagnosis. Struggles with communication and learning overcome through school, therapy, and personal growth.
Understanding the
importance of early
intervention in autism
spectrum disorder.
Exploring the impact of
family support and
dynamics on the journey
towards diagnosis.
Highlighting the challenges of communication and
learning faced by
individuals with autism.
Emphasizing the role of
specialized school
programs, therapy, and
personal development in
overcoming obstacles.
Celebrating the resilience and growth experienced
throughout the journey.

Chapter 2:
Navigating Mental Health (Pages 5-7)
This content provides a summary of the intersection of anxiety, stress eating, and coping mechanisms in the context of autism from a personal perspective. It explores personal insights, experiences, and strategies to navigate these challenges with

empathy and understanding. The focus is on the intricate relationship between anxiety, stress eating, and coping mechanisms within the realm of autism. Delve into the complex interplay between anxiety, stress eating, and coping mechanisms in the context of autism.

Offer personal anecdotes and reflections to shed light on navigating these challenges with compassion and insight.

Highlight the importance of understanding the unique dynamics at play in managing anxiety and stress eating for individuals on the autism spectrum.

enzo is my best friend and

friends

Heartwarming stories about the author's emotional support dog and the therapeutic value of animal companionship.

Animal companionship can provide comfort and emotional support during challenging times.

ll and they're really my best friends but Kenzo I miss a lot 's mentally sick and hope he's better and will I play with m Monopoly and we talk we

re together church, so yeah i really like each other so est friends I have multiple st friends, but these are my two best best friends

The bond between a person and their support animal can be incredibly strong and uplifting.

Pets have a unique ability to sense and respond to our emotions, providing a sense of connection and companionship.

Sharing heartwarming stories about the positive impact of emotional support animals can inspire others to consider the benefits of animal companionship. Exploring the profound impact of animal companionship on mental health and emotional wellbeing.

Highlighting the special bond between individuals and their emotional support animals.

Illustrating how pets can bring joy, comfort, and a sense of purpose into our lives.

Advocating for the recognition and importance of emotional support animals in promoting mental wellness.

Encouraging others to share their own uplifting experiences with animal companions to spread positivity and awareness.

Chapter 5: School
Explore author's educational journey,
challenges, impact of obstacles, effectiveness
of special education programs, and key
moments of growth.
Delve into the author's educational

background and the path they took to achieve their goals.

Highlight the challenges the author faced along the way and how they overcame them.

Discuss the impact of obstacles on the author's personal and academic growth.

Evaluate the effectiveness of special education programs in supporting the author's learning journey.

Reflect on key moments of growth and development that shaped the author's educational experience.

Embark on a journey through the author's educational experiences, from challenges to triumph.

Uncover the resilience and determination that propelled the author forward in the face of obstacles.

Examine how special education programs played a crucial role in shaping the author's learning path.

Capture the pivotal moments of growth that defined the author's educational narrative.

Illuminate the transformative power of overcoming adversity in educational pursuits.

Chapter 4: Therapy and Support

Sharing personal stories about therapy experiences and advocating for improved access to mental health resources.

By sharing personal stories, we can reduce stigma around mental health and encourage others to seek help.

Advocating for improved access to mental health resources can help make support more readily

available for those in need.

Together, we can create a more supportive and understanding community for mental health advocacy.

Empowering individuals to prioritize their mental
health and seek the support they deserve.
Encouraging open conversations about therapy
experiences to foster understanding and empathy. Collaborating to break down barriers and ensure
everyone has access to quality mental health
resources.
Building a compassionate community that values mental health and supports those on
their healing journey.
Chapter 6:
Hospitalization andRecovery
Reflections on hospitalization, treatment
experiences, and resilience narratives.
Exploring the emotional journey of
hospitalization and treatment experiences.
Highlighting stories of resilience and strength in
the face of adversity.
Sharing insights on coping mechanisms and
strategies during challenging times.
Reflecting on the impact of healthcare
environments on patient well-being.
Emphasizing the importance of empathy,
compassion, and support in healthcare settings.
Delving into the emotional rollercoaster of
hospitalization and treatment, capturing the
highs and lows of the journey.
Showcasing real-life accounts of individuals who
have shown remarkable resilience and courage in
the midst of their healthcare challenges.
Shedding light on effective coping mechanisms
and resilience-building strategies that have
helped individuals.navigate difficult times.
Examining how the design and atmosphere of
healthcare facilities can influence the emotional
and the mental well-being of patients.
Stressing the significance of fostering empathy,
compassion, and a supportive environment in
healthcare settings to enhance the overall
patient experience.

Chapter 7:
Returning Home
Discussions on readjustment, family support, and wellbeing strategies.
Exploring ways to adapt to change and readjust in different aspects of life.
Highlighting the importance of family support in maintaining mental and emotional well being. Sharing effective strategies for improving overall well being and coping with challenges.
Providing guidance on navigating life changes and finding ways to readjust effectively. Emphasizing the crucial role of family support in promoting mental and emotional wellness.
Offering practical tips and techniques for enhancing overall well-being and resilience in the face of adversity.
Fostering open dialogues on adapting to change and finding balance in various life areas.
Recognizing the vital role of family support in nurturing mental and emotional health. Offering valuable insights into enhancing overall well being and resilience through proactive strategies. Encouraging the exploration of readjustment processes and coping mechanisms in times of transition.
community
support, chapter 8
Promoting inclusivity, understanding, and empowerment for individuals with autism by establishing sensory-friendly environments, showcasing achievements, raising awareness of strengths, and advocating for equal opportunities and acceptance.
Creating safe and welcoming spaces that accommodate sensory sensitivities.
Designing environments that support independence and comfort for individuals with autism. Using calming colors, textures, and lighting to promote relaxation and reduce stress. Incorporating visual schedules and clear way finding to enhance understanding and communication.
Implementing quiet areas for retreat and sensory regulation.
Showcasing the talents and accomplishments of individuals with autism through thoughtful design elements.
Partnering with autism advocacy organizations to promote awareness and inclusivity in design practices.
Enhancing the quality of life for individuals with autism through thoughtful and intentional design choices.
Fostering a sense of belonging and empowerment through inclusive and sensory friendly environments.
Supporting independence and comfort by creating safe and welcoming spaces tailored to sensory sensitivities.

Promoting relaxation and reducing stress through the use of calming colors, textures, and lighting.
Improving communication and understanding with visual schedules and clear way findings elements.
Providing quiet retreat areas for sensory regulation and relaxation. Celebrating the talents and achievements of individuals with autism through purposeful design features.
Collaborating with autism advocacy organizations to advocate for awareness and inclusivity in design practices.

Page 30-31:
Chapter 20 -
Advocacy
Emphasizes the importance of raising awareness
to enhance care for individuals with autism.
Promotes understanding and acceptance of
individuals with autism.
Encourages inclusivity and support for those
with autism in various settings.
Advocates for creating sensory-friendly and safe
spaces for individuals with autism.
Highlights the value of early intervention and
specialized care for individuals with autism.
Raises awareness about the diverse strengths
and abilities of individuals with autism.
Fosters empathy and compassion towards
individuals with autism.
Encourages the creation of inclusive and
supportive communities for individuals with
autism.
Advocates for accessible resources and services
for individuals with autism and their families.
Promotes initiatives that promote
neurodiversity and celebrate the unique talents
of individuals with autism.
Encourages educators, caregivers, and the
general public to learn more about autism
spectrum disorder.
Collaborates with experts and organizations to

enhance support systems for individuals with
autism.
Aims to break stereotypes and misconceptions
surrounding autism.

Strength in
Vulnerability
Reflecting on vulnerability as strength, sharing struggles connects and empowers,
showcasing resilience, not weakness.
Embracing vulnerability as a source of strength and courage.
Finding power in sharing struggles and connecting with others.
Highlighting resilience as a symbol of inner strength and growth.
Shifting the narrative to showcase vulnerability as a sign of authenticity and courage.
Embracing vulnerability as a powerful tool for personal growth and connection.
Recognizing that sharing struggles can inspire and empower both ourselves and others.
Showcasing resilience as a testament to our inner strength and ability to overcome
challenges. Shifting perspectives to view vulnerability as a courageous act of
authenticity and self-acceptance.

Nature and Healing (Pages 68-70)
Nature's healing impact is explored, highlighting how
connecting with the natural world brings solace and
clarity during difficult times.
Incorporating design elements to bring
nature indoors.
Creating spaces that promote relaxation and stress
relief through natural materials and colors.
Designing indoor gardens or green walls to enhance
the connection with nature.
Utilizing natural light and views to improve mood
and productivity.
Incorporating water features for a calming effect.
Creating outdoor living spaces that blend
seamlessly with the natural surroundings.
Using sustainable materials to respect and protect
the environment.
Let's delve deeper into the concept of
design and its impact on our well-being, emphasizing
the importance of integrating nature into our living

spaces for a harmonious and serene environment:
By incorporating elements inspired by nature, we
can enhance our connection with the natural world
and create spaces that nurture our mental and
physical health.
Designing interiors that mimic natural environments
can reduce stress, improve cognitive function, and
foster a sense of tranquility.
Implementing design principles such as
natural materials, textures, and colors can evoke a
sense of calmness and rejuvenation in our
surroundings.
Integrating indoor plants, green walls, and botanical
motifs can bring the benefits of nature indoors,
promoting relaxation and enhancing air quality.
Maximizing natural light and views not only
brightens spaces but also uplifts our spirits and
boosts productivity.
Incorporating water features like fountains or indoor
ponds can introduce a soothing element that mimics
the calming effect of natural bodies of water.
Extending our living spaces outdoors to seamlessly
blend with nature allows us to immerse ourselves in
the beauty of the natural world and enjoy its
therapeutic benefits.
Embracing sustainable materials in our designs not
only minimizes our impact on the environment but
also fosters a deeper appreciation for nature's
resources and beauty.
The Barber
Connection
The author shares anecdotes about their sensory sensitivities and struggles with
grooming and personal care routines.
Exploring the challenges and triumphs of navigating sensory sensitivities in daily life.
Providing insights into the author's personal journey with grooming and self-care rituals.
Shedding light on the importance of understanding and accommodating sensory needs
in everyday routines.
Offering a compassionate perspective on the intersection of sensory experiences and
personal care habits.

Delving into the author's unique experiences with sensory sensitivities and how they impact grooming and personal care.
Offering a glimpse into the author's journey of overcoming challenges and finding success in self care routines.
Emphasizing the significance of recognizing and respecting sensory needs in day-to day activities. Presenting a compassionate view on how sensory sensitivities influence personal care practices.
Identity and
Struggles (Pages 29- 31)
Reflecting on personal identity, self-awareness, and the
path to self-acceptance.
Exploring how design can be a powerful tool for self
expression and introspection.
Using elements of color, texture, and layout to
reflect personal identity.
Creating spaces that promote self-awareness and
mindfulness.
Designing environments that nurture self
acceptance and self-love.
Incorporating meaningful objects and artwork that
resonate with your journey of self-discovery.
Embracing the journey of self-discovery through
thoughtful design choices.
Using design as a medium to express your true self
and inner emotions.
Crafting spaces that serve as a reflection of your
personal growth and aspirations.
Fostering a sense of harmony and balance in your
living environment to support your journey towards
self-acceptance.
Curating a space that not only looks beautiful but
also uplifts your spirit and encourages self-love.
Connecting
Through Creativity(Pages 86-88)
Delving into how creative expressions like art and music enhance connections.
Exploring the profound impact of creative outlets such as art and music on fostering connections and
deepening relationships.
Understanding how art and music serve as universal languages that transcend barriers

and bring people together.
Examining the role of creative expressions in
sparking meaningful conversations and shared
experiences.
Delving into how artistic collaborations and musical performances can strengthen
bonds and create
lasting memories.
Exploring how engaging in art and music can
cultivate empathy, understanding, and emotional
connections among individuals.
Reflecting on the power of creative outlets to bridge cultural divides and unite diverse
communities
through shared expressions of creativity.

Coping with Change (Pages 77-79)
Change is inevitable, and learning to cope with it is a significant aspect of resilience. I
share my experiences, strategies, and insights on adapting to life's inevitable
changes. Celebrating
Diversity (Pages 80- 82)
Celebrating neurodiversity, embracing differences, and fostering inclusivity to value and
respect individual uniqueness.
Promoting understanding and acceptance of diverse ways of thinking and being.
Creating spaces that accommodate various sensory needs and preferences.
Designing with flexibility to cater to different cognitive styles and abilities.
Incorporating calming elements for those sensitive to stimuli.
Ensuring accessibility for all individuals, regardless of their neurodiversity. Using
colors, textures, and layouts that promote a sense of safety and comfort for
everyone. Embracing the richness of diverse perspectives to inspire creativity and
innovation in design.

Dreams and
Aspirations
Dreams drive us forward by providing purpose and fulfillment through setting and
achieving goals, big and small.
Design plays a crucial role in turning dreams into reality by creating spaces that inspire
and motivate.
Through thoughtful design, we can transform environments to support our goals and
aspirations.
Design can help us visualize our dreams and create tangible steps towards achieving

them.
By incorporating elements that resonate with our aspirations, we can stay focused and motivated to pursue our dreams.
final thoughts
I plan on making a second book to see it and if you are, please watch it the TV show and like and subscribe dodo channel channel if you can and learn more about my youtube content and I have's podcast coming up soon and I plan on working on a movie and a book so see you later bye and I plan on making more content regarding autism and I'm actually autistic by the way my name is Logan Keener see y'all later Logan's experiences with therapy, the importance of a supportive network, and the journey towards self-discovery and empowerment. Emphasize the role of specialized programs, therapy, and personal development in overcoming obstacles.

Page 14-15: Chapter 5: School Experiences
- Navigate school environments as a person with autism, highlighting moments of growth, advocacy for inclusive education, and the power of resilience. Celebrate the resilience and growth experienced throughout the journey.

Page 16-17: Conclusion and Reflections
- Summarize key themes, insights, and lessons from Logan's life story. Encourage reflection on personal growth and experiences, fostering empathy and understanding.

Page 18-19: Acknowledgments
- Acknowledge individuals, organizations, and resources that have contributed to Logan's journey and the creation of this book.

Page 20-21: Additional Resources
- Provide a list of recommended books, websites, and resources related to autism, mental health, and personal growth for readers who want to explore further.

Page 22-23: Author's Note
- Include a personal note from Logan Keener, sharing gratitude, insights, or a message to readers about the book's purpose and impact.Sure, let's delve into your early and middle childhood experiences:

Early Childhood:
In Logan Keener's early years, the signs of autism spectrum disorder began to manifest. As a child, Logan navigated a world where communication and social interactions posed unique

challenges. Early childhood was a time of discovery for Logan and his family, as they sought answers and support to understand and address his needs effectively. Despite the initial struggles, Logan's early childhood was also marked by moments of curiosity, creativity, and a growing sense of self-awareness.

Middle Childhood:
As Logan transitioned into middle childhood, his experiences evolved alongside his understanding of autism and its impact on his daily life. Middle childhood brought new challenges in navigating social dynamics, academic settings, and personal development. Logan's journey during this period was shaped by supportive environments, specialized interventions, and the nurturing presence of family and friends. Middle childhood also marked significant milestones in Logan's growth, resilience, and gradual mastery of coping strategies to manage challenges associated with autism and mental health.

Throughout both early and middle childhood, Logan's story is a testament to the resilience, determination, and adaptability inherent in individuals navigating the complexities of autism spectrum disorder. His experiences highlight the importance of early intervention, supportive networks, and a personalized approach to education and therapy in fostering growth and well beingCertainly, let's explore Logan's experiences during his late teens, starting from the age of 12:

Late Teens: Adolescence and Transition
As Logan entered his late teens, the journey of self-discovery and personal growth continued amidst the challenges and opportunities of adolescence. Transitioning from childhood to adolescence marked a period of increased independence, self-awareness, and exploration of identity for Logan.

Academic and Social Dynamics:
During his late teens, Logan navigated the complexities of academic environments, forming friendships, and developing social skills. He encountered various educational settings, each presenting unique challenges and opportunities for growth. Through perseverance and determination, Logan gradually found his voice and established a sense of belonging within his peer group.

Navigating Mental Health:
The teenage years also brought a deeper understanding of mental health and well-being for Logan. He became more attuned to his emotions, coping mechanisms, and strategies for

managing anxiety and stress. Seeking support from trusted adults, therapists, and peer groups played a crucial role in Logan's journey of navigating mental health challenges effectively.

Exploring Interests and Passions:
As Logan matured, he explored his interests, passions, and talents, embracing opportunities for personal development and self-expression. Whether through creative outlets, hobbies, or extracurricular activities, Logan found avenues to channel his energy, creativity, and strengths.

Transition to teen hood:
Towards the latter years of his late teens, Logan began preparing for the transition to adulthood. This involved exploring post-secondary education options, vocational training, career pathways, and independent living skills. With the support of family, mentors, and community resources, Logan navigated this transition with resilience and determination.

Advocacy and Empowerment **Page 1: Title Page

Logan's Life Story

By Logan Keener

Page 2: Copyright Page

Copyright © Logan Keener 2024

Introduction

Table of contents

Chapter 1: The Beginning

Beginning with early experiences with autism, family dynamics, and the journey towards diagnosis. This chapter delves into the struggles with communication and learning that were overcome through school, therapy, and personal growth. It also highlights the importance of early intervention in autism spectrum disorder and explores the impact of family support and dynamics on the journey towards diagnosis.

Chapter 2: Navigating Mental Health

This chapter provides a summary of the intersection of anxiety, stress eating, and coping mechanisms in the context of autism from a personal perspective. It delves into personal insights, experiences, and strategies to navigate these challenges with empathy and understanding, emphasizing the unique dynamics at play in managing anxiety and stress eating for individuals on the autism spectrum.

Chapter 3: Kaiser Bear Keener: My Emotional Support

Heartwarming stories about the author's emotional support dog and the therapeutic value of animal companionship. It explores the profound impact of animal companionship on mental health and emotional well-being, advocating for the recognition and importance of emotional support animals in promoting mental wellness.

Chapter 4: Therapy and Support

This chapter shares personal stories about therapy experiences and advocates for improved access to mental health resources. By encouraging open conversations about therapy experiences and breaking down barriers, it aims to create a compassionate community that values mental health and supports those on their healing journey.

Chapter 5: School Experiences

Explore the author's educational journey, challenges, impact of obstacles, effectiveness of special education programs, and key moments of growth. Reflect on the transformative power of overcoming adversity in educational pursuits and the crucial role of special education programs in shaping the author's learning path.

Chapter 6: Hospitalization and Recovery

Reflections on hospitalization, treatment experiences, resilience narratives, and coping mechanisms during challenging times. Emphasizing the importance of empathy, compassion, and support in healthcare settings to enhance the overall patient experience.

Chapter 7: Returning Home

Discussions on readjustment, family support, and well-being strategies. Providing guidance on navigating life changes and finding ways to readjust effectively, with an emphasis on the crucial role of family support in promoting mental and emotional wellness.

Chapter 8: Community Support

Promoting inclusivity, understanding, and empowerment for individuals with autism by establishing sensory-friendly environments, showcasing achievements, raising awareness of strengths, and advocating for equal opportunities and acceptance.

Chapter 9: Advocacy

Emphasizes the importance of raising awareness, promoting understanding and acceptance, and advocating for accessible resources and services for individuals with autism and their families. Aims to break stereotypes and misconceptions surrounding autism.

Chapter 10: Strength in Vulnerability

Reflecting on vulnerability as strength, sharing struggles, connecting and empowering, showcasing resilience, and shifting the narrative to view vulnerability as a sign of authenticity and courage.

Chapter 11: Nature and Healing

Exploring nature's healing impact, incorporating biophilic design elements, and creating spaces that promote relaxation, stress relief, and connection with the natural world.

Chapter 12: The Barber Connection

Anecdotes about sensory sensitivities and struggles with grooming and personal care routines, highlighting the importance of understanding and accommodating sensory needs in everyday life.

Chapter 13: Identity and Struggles

Reflecting on personal identity, self-awareness, and the path to self-acceptance through thoughtful design choices that nurture self-awareness, self-acceptance, and self-love.

Chapter 14: Connecting Through Creativity

Delving into how creative expressions like art and music enhance connections, foster empathy, and bridge cultural divides through shared experiences of creativity.

Chapter 15: Coping with Change

Sharing experiences, strategies, and insights on adapting to life's inevitable changes as a significant aspect of resilience and personal growth.

Chapter 16: Celebrating Diversity

Celebrating neurodiversity, embracing differences, and fostering inclusivity through design practices that accommodate various sensory needs and preferences.

Chapter 17: Dreams and Aspirations

Exploring how design plays a crucial role in turning dreams into reality by creating spaces that inspire, motivate, and support goals and aspirations.

Final Thoughts

Plans for future content regarding autism, including a second book, a TV show, a podcast, a movie, and continued advocacy and awareness efforts.

Page 30-31: Chapter 20 - Advocacy

Emphasizes the importance of raising awareness, promoting understanding and acceptance, and advocating for accessible resources and services for individuals with autism and their families. Aims to break stereotypes and misconceptions surrounding autism.

Strength in Vulnerability

Reflecting on vulnerability as strength, sharing struggles, connecting and empowering, showcasing resilience, and shifting the narrative to view vulnerability as a sign of authenticity and courage.

Nature and Healing

Exploring nature's healing impact, incorporating biophilic design elements, and creating spaces that promote relaxation, stress relief, and connection with the natural world.

The Barber Connection

Anecdotes about sensory sensitivities and struggles with grooming and personal care routines, highlighting the importance of understanding and accommodating sensory needs in everyday life.

Identity and Struggles

Reflecting on personal identity, self-awareness, and the path to self-acceptance through thoughtful design choices that nurture self-awareness, self-acceptance, and self-love.

Connecting Through Creativity

Delving into how creative expressions like art and music enhance connections, foster empathy, and bridge cultural divides through shared experiences of creativity.

Coping with Change

Sharing experiences, strategies, and insights on adapting to life's inevitable changes as a significant aspect of resilience and personal growth.

Celebrating Diversity

Celebrating neurodiversity, embracing differences, and fostering inclusivity through design practices that accommodate various sensory needs and preferences.

Dreams and Aspirations

Exploring how design plays a crucial role in turning dreams into reality by creating spaces that inspire, motivate, and support goals and aspirations.

Final Thoughts

Plans for future content regarding autism, including a second book, a TV show, a podcast, a movie, and continued advocacy and awareness efforts.

Chapter 18: Middle Childhood Journey

In the midst of middle childhood, Logan Keener embarked on a remarkable journey of transformation. From the challenges of low-functioning autism to navigating a path of improved functioning, this period was marked by resilience, growth, and significant milestones.

During early middle childhood, Logan faced various obstacles associated with low-functioning autism. Communication difficulties, social interactions, and sensory sensitivities posed significant challenges, requiring dedicated support and intervention. Through the dedication of caregivers, therapists, and educators, gradual progress began to emerge.

Therapeutic interventions, structured learning environments, and personalized support played crucial roles in fostering development and building essential skills. Speech therapy, occupational therapy, and behavioral interventions were instrumental in enhancing communication abilities, sensory processing, and social interaction skills.

As middle childhood progressed, Logan experienced notable improvements in communication, socialization, and daily functioning. Increased language fluency, better social understanding, and improved emotional regulation were evident signs of progress and growth. These achievements not only reflected personal resilience but also highlighted the effectiveness of early interventions and tailored support systems.

Transitioning into late childhood brought forth new challenges and opportunities. The onset of adolescence often comes with a myriad of changes, both internal and external. Hormonal fluctuations, social dynamics, academic demands, and self-identity exploration added layers of complexity to Logan's journey.

Navigating the ups and downs of late childhood required adaptability, self-awareness, and coping strategies. Managing heightened emotions, peer relationships, and academic expectations became focal points of growth and adaptation. The process of understanding oneself, developing autonomy, and navigating social landscapes became integral aspects of this transformative phase.

Despite the challenges, Logan demonstrated resilience, determination, and a positive outlook. Learning to embrace strengths, seek support when needed, and navigate challenges with courage and perseverance were key themes during late childhood. Building resilience through setbacks, celebrating achievements, and fostering a sense of self-worth contributed to personal growth and development.

As late childhood progressed, Logan gradually acclimated to the complexities of adolescence. Developing a sense of identity, cultivating friendships, pursuing interests, and setting goals became foundational elements of this phase. While there were moments of uncertainty and adjustment, there were also moments of joy, accomplishment, and self-discovery.

Looking back on the middle childhood journey, Logan acknowledges the transformative power of resilience, support, and personal growth. Each challenge navigated, each milestone achieved, and each lesson learned contributed to a stronger sense of self and a deeper understanding of the journey with autism.

Feel free to add more details or adjust the content further based on your experiences and perspective!

Chapter 18: Middle Childhood Journey

In the midst of middle childhood, Logan Keener embarked on a remarkable journey of transformation. From the challenges of low-functioning autism to navigating a path of improved functioning, this period was marked by resilience, growth, and significant milestones.

During early middle childhood, Logan faced various obstacles associated with low-functioning autism. Communication difficulties, social interactions, and sensory sensitivities posed significant challenges, requiring dedicated support and intervention. Through the dedication of caregivers, therapists, and educators, gradual progress began to emerge.

Therapeutic interventions, structured learning environments, and personalized support played crucial roles in fostering development and building essential skills. Speech therapy, occupational therapy, and behavioral interventions were instrumental in enhancing communication abilities, sensory processing, and social interaction skills.

As middle childhood progressed, Logan experienced notable improvements in communication, socialization, and daily functioning. Increased language fluency, better social understanding, and improved emotional regulation were evident signs of progress and growth. These achievements not only reflected personal resilience but also highlighted the effectiveness of early interventions and tailored support systems.

Transitioning into late childhood brought forth new challenges and opportunities. The onset of adolescence often comes with a myriad of changes, both internal and external. Hormonal fluctuations, social dynamics, academic demands, and self-identity exploration added layers of complexity to Logan's journey.

Navigating the ups and downs of late childhood required adaptability, self-awareness, and coping strategies. Managing heightened emotions, peer relationships, and academic expectations became focal points of growth and adaptation. The process of understanding oneself, developing autonomy, and navigating social landscapes became integral aspects of this transformative phase.

Despite the challenges, Logan demonstrated resilience, determination, and a positive outlook. Learning to embrace strengths, seek support when needed, and navigate challenges with courage and perseverance were key themes during late childhood. Building resilience through setbacks, celebrating achievements, and fostering a sense of self-worth contributed to personal growth and development.

As late childhood progressed, Logan gradually acclimated to the complexities of adolescence. Developing a sense of identity, cultivating friendships, pursuing interests, and setting goals became foundational elements of this phase. While there were moments of uncertainty and adjustment, there were also moments of joy, accomplishment, and self-discovery.

Looking back on the middle childhood journey, Logan acknowledges the transformative power of resilience, support, and personal growth. Each challenge navigated, each milestone achieved, and each lesson learned contributed to a stronger sense of self and a deeper understanding of the journey with autism.

Feel free to add more details or adjust the content further based on your experiences and perspective!

By logan Keener